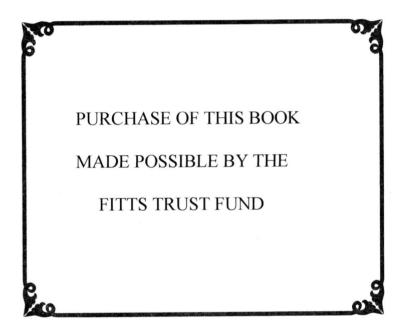

PURCHASE OF THIS BOOK

MADE POSSIBLE BY THE

FITTS TRUST FUND

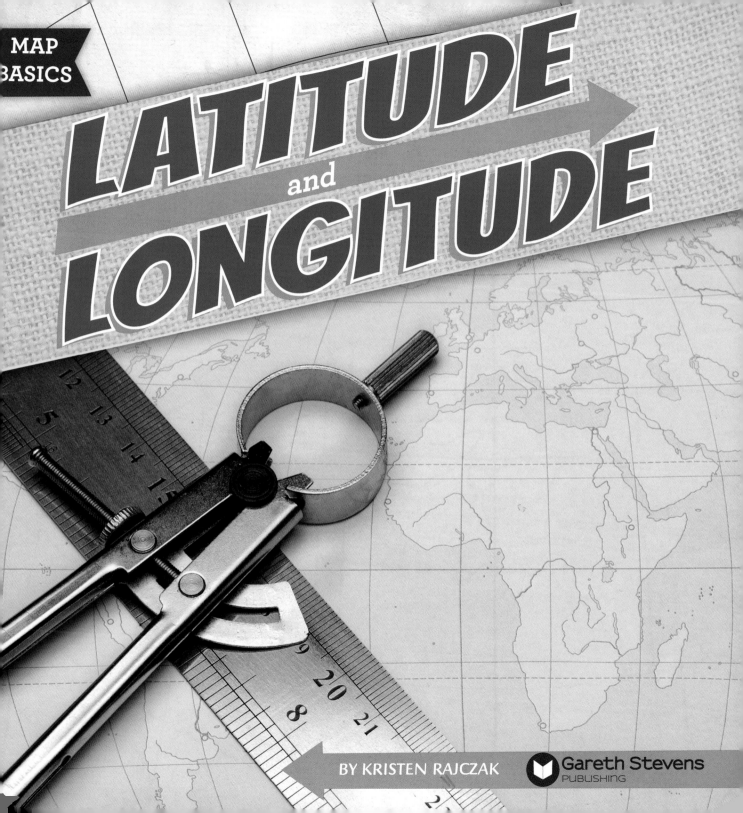

LATITUDE
and
LONGITUDE

BY KRISTEN RAJCZAK

Gareth Stevens
PUBLISHING

Please visit our website, www.garethstevens.com. For a free color catalog of all our high-quality books, call toll free 1-800-542-2595 or fax 1-877-542-2596.

Library of Congress Cataloging-in-Publication Data

Rajczak, Kristen.
Latitude and longitude / by Kristen Rajczak.
 p. cm. — (Map basics)
Includes index.
ISBN 978-1-4824-1079-2 (pbk.)
ISBN 978-1-4824-1080-8 (6-pack)
ISBN 978-1-4824-1078-5 (library binding)
1. Latitude — Juvenile literature. 2. Longitude — Juvenile literature. I. Rajczak, Kristen. II. Title.
QB224.5 R35 2014
526—d23

First Edition

Published in 2015 by
Gareth Stevens Publishing
111 East 14th Street, Suite 349
New York, NY 10003

Copyright © 2015 Gareth Stevens Publishing

Designer: Sarah Liddell
Editor: Kristen Rajczak

Photo credits: Cover, p. 1, Galushko Sergey/Shutterstock.com; p. 5 Frank Ramspott/iStock Vectors/ Getty Images; p. 7 (Earth) MarcelClemens/Shutterstock.com; p. 7 (angle) Radu Bercan/ Shutterstock.com; p. 9 Agrus/Shutterstock.com; p. 11 (main) Vilainecrevette/Shutterstock.com; p. 11 (globe) Peter Hermes Furian/Shutterstock.com; p. 13 (main) lexaarts/Shutterstock.com; p. 13 (Galileo) Omikron/Yerkes Observatory/Photo Researchers/Getty Images; p. 15 iconspro/ Shutterstock.com; pp. 17, 19 (map) magicinfoto/Shutterstock.com; p. 19 (main) Blend Images/ DreamPictures/Vetta/Getty Images; p. 21 PILart/Shutterstock.com.

Printed in the United States of America

CPSIA compliance information: Batch #CS15GS: For further information contact Gareth Stevens, New York, New York at 1-800-542-2595.

CONTENTS

Words in the glossary appear in **bold** type the first time they are used in the text.

GLOBAL ADDRESS

Imagine you're visiting China and someone asks you where you live. Giving them your street address won't be helpful since they don't know your hometown. You could tell them the state or country, but that's not exactly where you live. And what if others around you don't speak English and can't understand?

Every place on Earth has a **global** address. The numbers that make up a global address are **coordinates** on the grid of imaginary lines used on maps and globes to help us find places on Earth.

JUST THE FACTS
It's important for the coordinates of global addresses to be numbers because then everyone on Earth can understand them, no matter what language they speak.

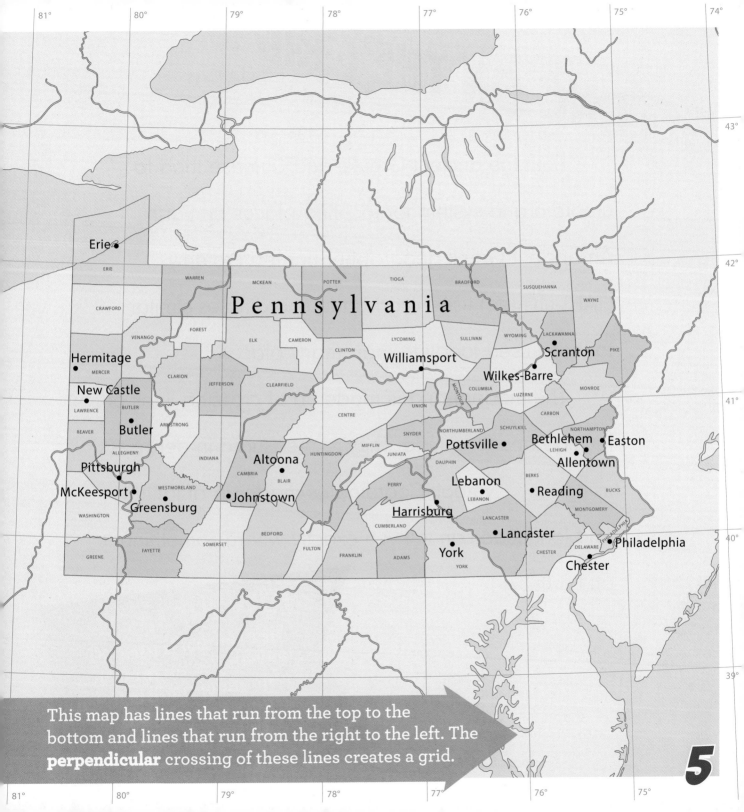

This map has lines that run from the top to the bottom and lines that run from the right to the left. The **perpendicular** crossing of these lines creates a grid.

5

GETTING ON THE GRID

Both the ancient Greeks and Chinese tried to create a grid system for locating places on Earth. An ancient Greek geographer named Ptolemy (TAHL-uh-mee) used a grid and coordinates similar to those used today to map many places.

The modern grid is made up of crossing lines of latitude and longitude. They're measured in degrees using the ° symbol. Coordinates made up of latitude and longitude can tell you exactly where something is on Earth.

JUST THE FACTS

The ° symbol is used to show angles. An angle is the amount of space between two lines that intersect, or cross each other.

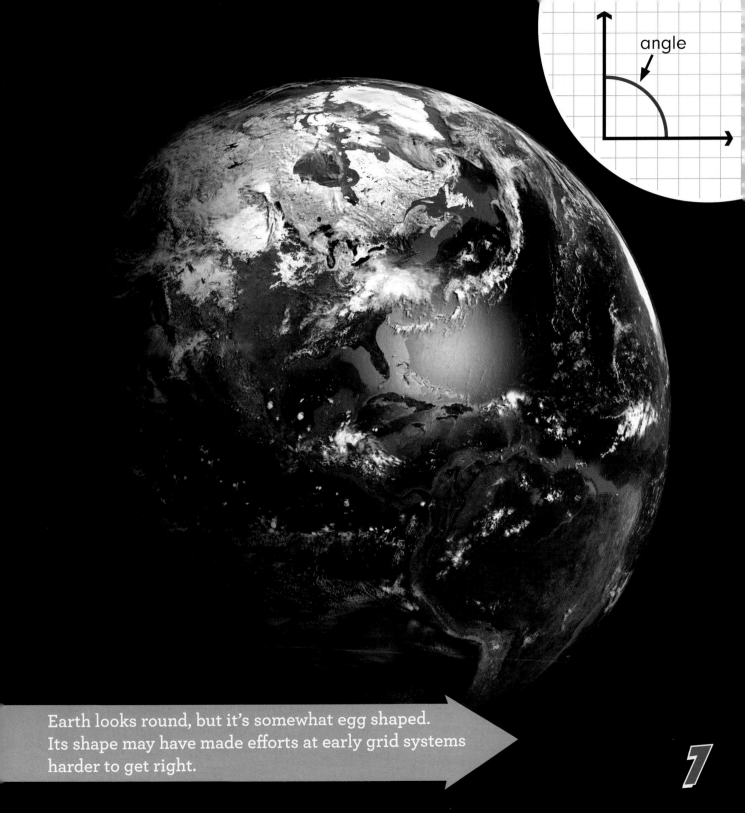

angle

Earth looks round, but it's somewhat egg shaped.
Its shape may have made efforts at early grid systems
harder to get right.

THE EQUATOR

The equator is the most important line of latitude. It's the imaginary line that runs around Earth's center, splitting the planet into two halves, or hemispheres. The Northern Hemisphere is above the equator, and the Southern Hemisphere is below it. Every part of the equator is equally **distant** from the North Pole and the South Pole.

Even the earliest maps had the equator marked on them. Geographers, scientists, and travelers had long used the sun to chart location, and the equator gets the most sun of any place on Earth.

JUST THE FACTS

The equator is the longest line of latitude. It's 24,901.55 miles (40,075.2 km) long and runs through Indonesia, Ecuador, and Brazil, among other countries.

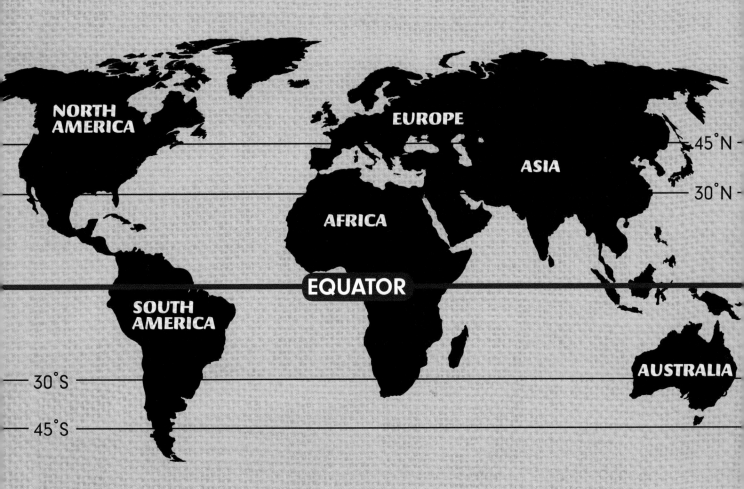

NORTH
AMERICA

EUROPE

45°N

ASIA

30°N

AFRICA

EQUATOR

SOUTH
AMERICA

AUSTRALIA

30°S

45°S

Nearness to the equator is one of the key causes of a place's climate, or the average weather conditions of a place. The closer to the equator an area is, the more sun it gets.

9

PERFECT PARALLELS

Because lines of latitude run **parallel** to each other, they're called parallels. Parallels run east and west above and below the equator. They show how far north or south a place is.

Latitude coordinates fall between 0° and 90°. They're a measurement of the angle created when you draw a line from the center of Earth to the equator and a line from the center of Earth to the parallel. The number will be higher the farther you get from the equator, which is 0° latitude.

JUST THE FACTS

A latitude coordinate will have a + before it or "N" after it if it's a northern parallel. A southern parallel will begin with − or have "S" after it.

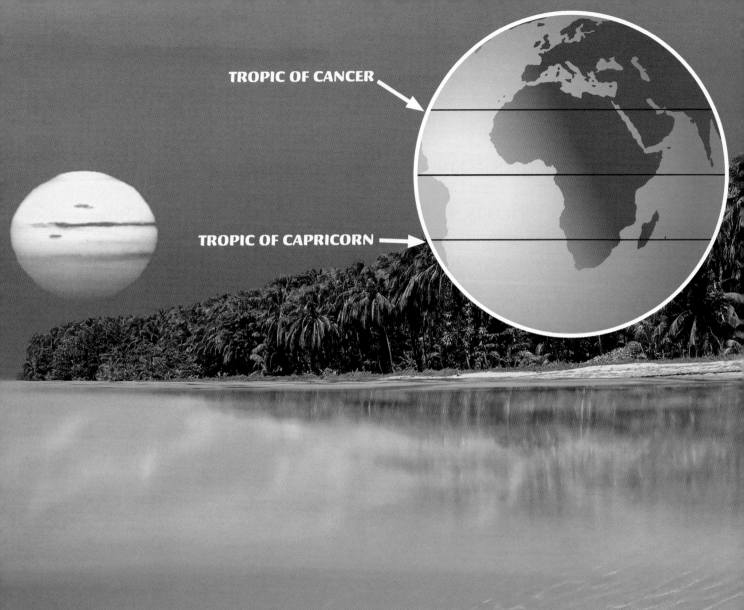

TROPIC OF CANCER

TROPIC OF CAPRICORN

The Tropic of Cancer is found at 23.5°N latitude and gets direct sun at the summer **solstice**. The Tropic of Capricorn is found at 23.5°S latitude and gets direct sun during the winter solstice. The area between these parallels is called the tropics.

MEASURING LONGITUDE

Longitude lines are used to show how far east or west a place is. In the 1600s, Galileo figured out how to measure longitude using a ship's local time and the time at its home port.

Earth completes its full 360° **rotation** in 24 hours. That means a given point on the planet moves 15° of longitude each hour. The difference between local time and the time at a ship's home port showed how many degrees of longitude a ship had traveled.

JUST THE FACTS

Galileo used the moons of Jupiter to figure out what time it was aboard a ship.

Galileo

Lines of longitude and latitude are imaginary mapping tools. Lines of longitude have been added to this photograph of Earth, taken from space, to help find places on the globe and show how Earth moves.

Since the equator was already a recognized imaginary line on maps, it made sense to use it as the 0° base of other parallels. Choosing a line of 0° longitude wasn't as easy.

In 1884, a group of nations set the Prime Meridian as the longitude line that passes through Greenwich, England. Lines of longitude, or meridians, run from the North Pole to the South Pole to the east and west of the Prime Meridian. They're also measured in degrees that range from 0° to 180°.

JUST THE FACTS

At 180° longitude lies the International Date Line. This is the longitude line chosen to mark the place where each calendar day begins.

GREENWICH, ENGLAND

PRIME MERIDIAN

A longitude coordinate is marked by "E" or + for east, and "W" or – for west to note what direction away from the Prime Meridian the line is.

The map of the United States on the next page has latitude lines running from right to left and longitude lines running from top to bottom. On each line is a number. That's the measurement of the parallel or meridian in degrees.

To give the location of a place, you need to use the measurement both of latitude and longitude. When writing coordinates, the latitude measurement comes first. Can you find which lines of latitude and longitude intersect on the state of New Jersey?

JUST THE FACTS
Coordinates work two ways. You can use a map to find the coordinates of a certain place. Or someone can give you coordinates of a place and you can use a map to locate it.

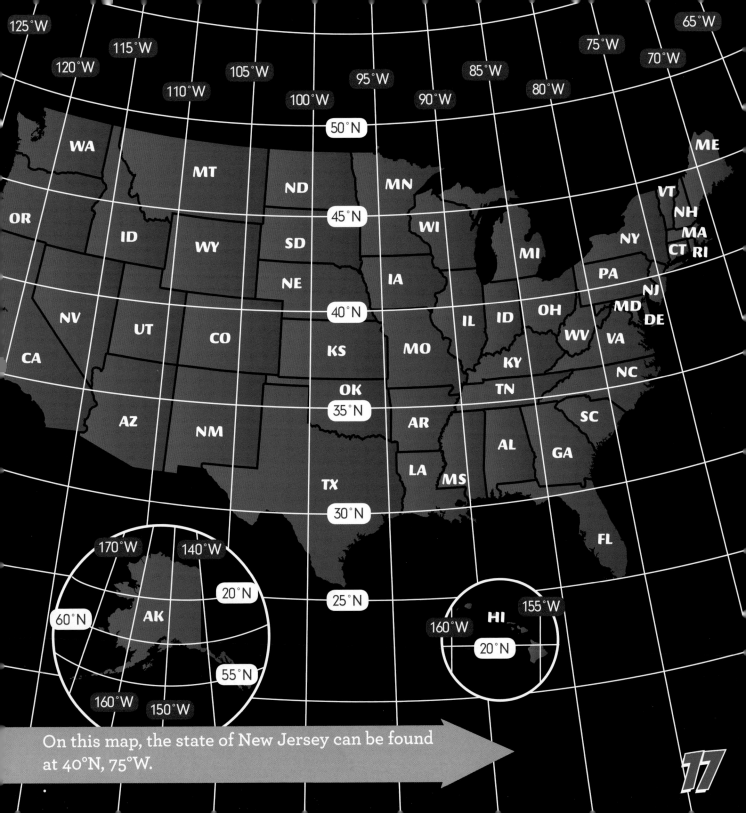

On this map, the state of New Jersey can be found at 40°N, 75°W.

17

One of the coolest features of using coordinates is **accuracy**. Remember finding New Jersey on page 17? The intersection of latitude and longitude on that map told you where, roughly, the state is on the globe. What if you wanted to find exactly where the city of Dallas, Texas, is?

Degrees of latitude and longitude are broken down into smaller units of minutes and seconds. They show just how close to a meridian or parallel a place is.

JUST THE FACTS

There are 60 minutes in one degree and 60 seconds in one minute. Minutes are shown by the symbol ' and seconds are shown by ":

Using degrees, minutes, and seconds, you cannot only find Dallas—you can give the coordinates of a certain building in the city! Dallas is found at 32°46'33" N, 96°47'48" W.

Today, many people have a global positioning system (GPS) on their cell phone or in their car. While you can always input an address when using a GPS, it can also recognize coordinates! This can be helpful if you're driving or biking through a park or the mountains, or canoeing down a river.

Understanding latitude and longitude coordinates can help you meet your friends at a certain bend in the river. Map reading can help you find your way back to a main road, too.

JUST THE FACTS

Coordinates are important in another hobby, too—geocaching! Groups use the Internet to find sets of coordinates. They follow a map or GPS to the spot and find notes, objects, or treasures other geocachers have left behind.

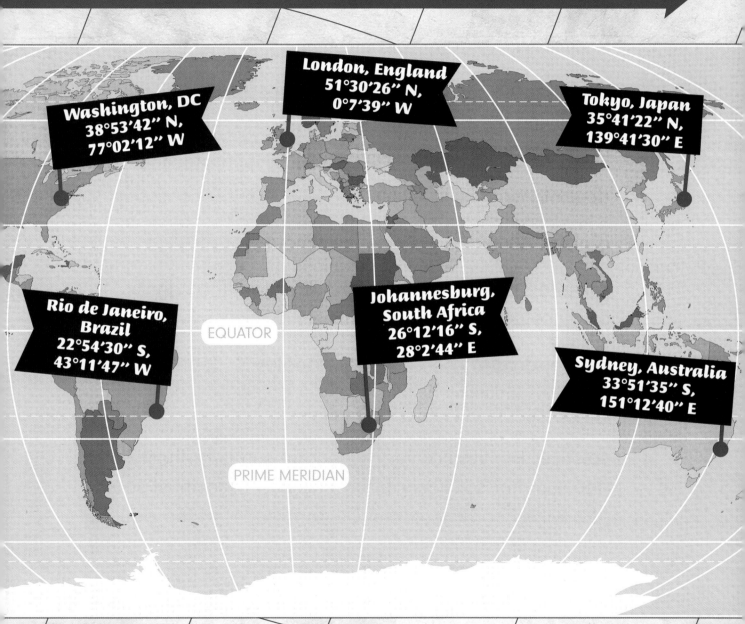

COORDINATES OF MAJOR CITIES

Washington, DC
38°53'42" N,
77°02'12" W

London, England
51°30'26" N,
0°7'39" W

Tokyo, Japan
35°41'22" N,
139°41'30" E

Rio de Janeiro,
Brazil
22°54'30" S,
43°11'47" W

EQUATOR

Johannesburg,
South Africa
26°12'16" S,
28°2'44" E

Sydney, Australia
33°51'35" S,
151°12'40" E

PRIME MERIDIAN

GLOSSARY

accuracy: freedom from error

coordinate: any of a set of numbers used in specifying the location of a point on a line, on a plane, or in space

distant: far off

global: having to do with the whole world

parallel: running in the same direction, the same distance apart, and never meeting

perpendicular: being at right angles

rotation: the act of turning

solstice: the time of year when the sun is farthest north (the summer solstice, about June 21), or farthest south (the winter solstice, about December 21) of the equator

BOOKS

Block, Marta Segal, and Daniel R. Block. *Reading Maps.* Chicago, IL: Heinemann Library, 2008.

Olien, Rebecca. *Longitude and Latitude.* New York, NY: Children's Press, 2013.

WEBSITES

ABCya! Latitude and Longitude Game
www.abcya.com/latitude_and_longitude_practice.htm
Practice your map skills in this treasure hunting game.

The Equator and Prime Meridian
www.socialstudiesforkids.com/articles/geography/equatorprimemeridian.htm
Read more about the equator and Prime Meridian, and find links to other geography topics.

INDEX